CANDLE
Day by Day
Walk with Jesus

by Juliet David
illustrated by Jane Heyes

CANDLE
BOOKS

To the reader

Who is Jesus? Why is he so special?

What happened when Jesus lived here on earth?
Did he do miracles? Did he heal people?

Why was Jesus killed? Was that the end?

These and many other questions are answered in this book, which retells
simply and clearly the main events of Jesus' birth, life, and death.

The story is closely based on the accounts given in the four Gospels –
Matthew, Mark, Luke, and John – in the New Testament part of the Bible.

During 40 days' reading you will meet Jesus and his friends,
and discover the wonderful story of his life.

Published by Candle Books
an imprint of
Lion Hudson plc
Wilkinson House, Jordan Hill Road,
Oxford OX2 8DR, England
www.lionhudson.com/candle

ISBN 978 1 78128 291 5
e-ISBN 978 1 78128 313 4

First edition 2016

A catalogue record for this book
is available from the British Library

Printed and bound in Malaysia,
April 2016, LH18

Acknowledgments
Scripture quotations marked CEV are
taken or adapted from the Contemporary
English Version copyright © 1991, 1992,
1995 by American Bible Society. Used by
permission.

Scripture quotations marked NLT are taken
or adapted from the Holy Bible, New Living
Translation, copyright © 1996 by Tyndale
House Foundation. Used by permission
of Tyndale House Publishers, Inc., Carol
Stream, Illinois 60188. All rights reserved.

Scripture quotations marked NIV are taken
or adapted from the Holy Bible, New
International Version® NIV® Copyright ©
1973, 1978, 1984 by Biblica, Inc.® Used by
permission. All rights reserved worldwide.
The "NIV" and "New International Version"
are trademarks registered in the United
States Patent and Trademark Office by
Biblica, Inc.® Use of either trademark
requires the permission of Biblica, Inc.®

Scripture quotations marked NRSV are
taken or adapted from the New Revised
Standard Version Bible: Anglicized Edition,
copyright © 1989, 1995 National Council of
the Churches of Christ in the United States
of America. Used by permission. All rights
reserved.

Scripture quotations marked REB are taken
or adapted from the Revised English Bible,
copyright © Oxford University Press and
Cambridge University Press 1989. All rights
reserved.

Scripture quotations marked NJB are taken
or adapted from The New Jerusalem Bible,
copyright © 1985 by Darton, Longman
& Todd Ltd. and Doubleday, a division
of Random House, Inc. Reproduced by
permission. All rights reserved.

Scripture quotations marked GNB are taken
or adapted from the Good News Bible ©
1994 published by the Bible Societies/
HarperCollins Publishers Ltd UK, Good
News Bible © American Bible Society 1966,
1971, 1976, 1992. Used with permission.

Contents

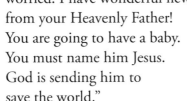

Mary said,
"With all my
heart I praise
the Lord."

Luke 1:46 CEV

How do you
think Mary felt
when the angel
appeared?

Mary's visitor

A young woman named Mary lived in the little town of Nazareth. One day the angel Gabriel visited her.

Mary was amazed – and a bit frightened.

"Mary!" said the angel. "There's no need to be worried. I have wonderful news from your Heavenly Father! You are going to have a baby. You must name him Jesus. God is sending him to save the world."

Mary was puzzled.

"How can this happen?" she asked. "I'm not married yet."

"God will make this happen," said Gabriel. "With God, nothing is impossible."

"I will do whatever God wants!" said Mary.

A long journey

Mary loved a kind and good man named Joseph, the village carpenter. They were engaged to be married.

So Mary and Joseph got married straight away.

Near the time for Mary's baby to be born, soldiers nailed up a notice in Nazareth. It said: "Everyone must go back to the town where they were born, to register their name."

Joseph and Mary had to travel to Joseph's home town, Bethlehem, many miles away.

They set out on the long, tiring journey.

At last they arrived.

Because Joseph was a descendant of King David, he had to go to Bethlehem in Judea, David's ancient home.

Luke 2:4 NLT

Where did they stay that night?

5

A baby is born

Mary wrapped him in cloths and placed him in a manger, because there was no room for them in the inn.

Luke 2:7 NIV

The Son of God was born in a borrowed stable.

Joseph found an inn and knocked on the door.

"I'm sorry," said the innkeeper. "We're full! But I do have a little stable," he added. "You could sleep there."

And in that stable, among the donkeys and cows, Mary's precious baby was born.

Mary looked at him lovingly.

She wrapped her baby around and around, in a long piece of soft cloth.

Joseph put clean straw in the animals' feed box.

"I've made a little bed for baby Jesus," he said.

Joseph laid the baby gently in the manger.

Soon little Jesus was fast asleep on the straw.

"The Messiah...
has been born
tonight in
Bethlehem, the
city of David!"

Luke 2:11 NLT

**Who were the
first people to
hear that Jesus
was born?**

The angel's message

In fields outside Bethlehem shepherds were minding
their sheep.

Suddenly, a bright light shone down.

The shepherds felt really scared.

"Don't be frightened!" said the angel.
"I have good news that will bring joy to all people!
Tonight your king has been born in Bethlehem.
You will find him lying in a manger.
Go – see for yourselves!"

At the stable

The shepherds rushed off into Bethlehem to search for the baby king. Soon they found the little stable.

They peered inside and saw Mary, Joseph, and baby Jesus lying in a manger.

They all crowded in to look at the baby. Then the shepherds knelt down.

They told Mary and Joseph excitedly what the angel had told them.

Then, noticing Mary was very tired, the shepherds crept out and went back to look after their sheep.

Mary kept thinking about everything they had said.

As the shepherds returned to their sheep, they were praising God and saying wonderful things about him.

Luke 2:20 CEV

What do you think the shepherds told their friends about this night?

"A ruler will
come from
Bethlehem
who will be
the shepherd
for my people
Israel."

Matthew 2:6
NLT

*Does the Bible
tell us how
many wise men
followed the
star?*

A new star

Far away in the East lived some very
wise men who studied the stars.

Late one night one of them
exclaimed, "I've never seen
that star before!"

"It's a special sign," said
another. "It means a new
king has been born."

"Then we must follow this star
and find him," they all agreed.

So the wise men set out on a long journey,
following the special, new star.

Crossing deserts and wastelands, hills and valleys,
the wise men came at last to Bethlehem.

A new king

Finally the star stopped over the house in Bethlehem where young Jesus was.

Inside, they found Jesus with his mother, Mary.

When the wise men saw Jesus, they knelt before him.

They had brought with them costly presents: gold and precious scents, called frankincense and myrrh. They set down their gifts for the little boy.

Presents fit for a king!

When the wise men saw the star, they were filled with joy!

Matthew 2:10
NLT

What happened next to the wise men?

The child Jesus grew. He became strong and wise, and God blessed him.

Luke 2:40 CEV

Jesus learned to read the books of the Law that Moses had written.

Jesus grows up

Mary and Joseph took Jesus back to Nazareth, where they had lived before Jesus was born.

Jesus grew up with Mary and Joseph in this little town. Joseph worked as a carpenter, and Jesus helped him in his workshop, sawing and hammering.

When he was old enough, Jesus started to go to school. He listened carefully to the lessons and remembered everything he was taught.

How proud his mother Mary was!

Jesus visits Jerusalem

Once a year the Jewish people celebrated the great Passover festival. They loved to go to Jerusalem, where the great Temple stood.

When Jesus was twelve years old, Mary said, "This year you can come with us."

When they arrived in Jerusalem, Mary, Joseph, and Jesus went to the Temple to worship.

"This is the house of God, my Heavenly Father," thought Jesus. There he met wise men and priests.

Too soon they started the long walk back to Nazareth.

Mary didn't see Jesus all day.

Every year Jesus' parents went to Jerusalem for the festival of Passover.

Luke 2:41 NRSV

All who heard Jesus were amazed at his understanding and his answers.

Luke 2:47 NRSV

What did Jesus' answer to Mary mean?

Mary finds Jesus

Nobody seemed to have seen Jesus since they had left Jerusalem. Mary and Joseph felt worried.

"We need to go back," said Joseph.

So back they went to Jerusalem.

But still they didn't find Jesus.

"There's only one place left to look for Jesus," said Mary in desperation, "– the Temple."

There they found Jesus! He had been asking the priests and wise men questions. The old men were amazed this boy knew so much about the Law of God.

"We've been looking everywhere for you," said Mary. "We were *really* worried."

"I had to come to my Father's house, to learn the things I need to know," said Jesus.

This time Jesus did set off home with Mary and Joseph.

Cousin John

Jesus' cousin, John, lived in the desert. He wore clothes made of rough camel's hair.

Big crowds of people came to hear John. He told them, "You do a lot of bad things. Turn around and start doing what's right. Be baptized! That way, you can make a fresh start."

Many people said they were sorry for the wrong things they'd done.

John baptized them in the River Jordan. He dipped them under the water. When they came out, they felt as if they had been born again.

People called him "John the Baptist".

In many different ways John preached the good news to the people.

Luke 3:18 CEV

Why did so many people come to listen to John?

Jesus is baptized

As soon as Jesus came out of the water, he saw the sky open and the Holy Spirit coming down to him like a dove.

Mark 1:10 CEV

Who was it speaking after Jesus was baptized?

Some people came and asked John, "Are you the person God is sending to save us?"

"Someone much greater than me is coming," John said. "I'm not fit even to undo his sandals!"

Soon after, Jesus came to John.

"Please baptize me," said Jesus.

"But Jesus, *you* should be baptizing me," said John. "There's no way *I* should be baptizing you!"

"This is what God wants!" Jesus replied.

So John agreed. He dipped Jesus in the River Jordan.

When Jesus came out of the water, a voice from heaven said, "This is my own dear Son. I am very pleased with him!"

17

Jesus told Simon, "From now on you will bring in people instead of fish."

Luke 5:10 CEV

Jesus chooses a team

One day Jesus noticed four fishermen mending their nets beside Lake Galilee.

They were Peter and his brother Andrew, James and his twin brother John.

"Follow me!" said Jesus. "Then I will teach you how to catch people instead of fish!"

At once the fishermen pulled their boats up the beach, left everything, and followed Jesus.

They became the first of Jesus' special friends, the "disciples".

Sometimes we call Jesus' disciples his "apostles".

18

Jesus calls a taxman

People didn't like tax collectors. They swindled people and took too much money.

One day Jesus saw a taxman named Matthew working at his desk.

"Follow me!" Jesus called to him.

At once Matthew got up, left his work and his money, and followed Jesus. He became one of Jesus' disciples.

The twelve disciples were Peter and Andrew, James and John, Philip, Bartholomew, Thomas, Matthew, another man also named James, Thaddaeus, Simon, and Judas Iscariot.

*Jesus said,
"I didn't come
to invite good
people to turn
to God.
I came to invite
sinners."*

Luke 5:32 CEV

Jesus chose twelve disciples. They came from different places and had different skills.

19

*Jesus saw how
much faith they
had.*

Luke 5:20 CEV

Imagine if
someone made
a hole in the
roof of your
house and let
down a sick
person!

Through the roof!

A man who couldn't walk wanted Jesus to heal him.

So four of his friends carried him on a stretcher to the house where Jesus was teaching.

When they saw the huge crowds there, they lifted the stretcher onto the flat roof of the house. Then they tore a hole in the roof and lowered the stretcher down in front of Jesus.

Stand up!

Jesus said to the man, "I forgive your sins."

Some of the religious leaders said, "*Who* does he think he is? Only God can forgive sin."

"Which is harder – to forgive sin or to heal sickness?" asked Jesus. "I can do both!"

Then Jesus said to the man, "Stand up! You are well."

The man jumped to his feet, picked up his stretcher, and hurried home.

Everyone was amazed and gave praise to God.

Luke 5:26 NIV

Do you think this man's friends believed Jesus could heal him?

21

*"God blesses
those people
whose hearts
are pure. They
will see him!"*

Matthew 5:8 CEV

Sometimes
people call
these sayings
of Jesus the
"Sermon on
the Mount".

Jesus' way

Jesus often went to the hills around the Sea of Galilee. One day a crowd followed him, to hear him teaching and telling stories.

Jesus explained about the good things God gives us.

"God blesses those people who trust only in him," he said. "God blesses people who are humble.

"Happy are people who want to do God's wishes.

"Forgive other people and you will be forgiven.

"People who work for peace shall be called God's children.

"Be happy; you will have a great reward in heaven."

How to pray

One of Jesus' friends asked him,
"Lord, how should we pray?"
  So Jesus taught them how to pray.
  "Go somewhere quiet when you want to pray
to God. He knows exactly what you need.
This is how you should pray to him:

  "Our Father in heaven,
    May your holy name be respected;
    May your kingdom come;
    May your will be done on earth,
      as it is in heaven.
    Give us today the food we need.
    Forgive us the wrongs we have done,
    As we forgive the wrongs
      that others have done to us.
    Do not bring us to the point of
      temptation,
    But keep us safe from evil."

Based on Matthew 6:9–13 GNB

"When you pray, don't talk on and on as people do who don't know God."

Matthew 6:7 CEV

We often call this prayer "The Lord's Prayer".

Asleep in a boat

*A great gale
arose, and the
waves beat into
the boat.*

Mark 4:37 NRSV

Jesus was with his disciples beside Lake Galilee.
He had been telling some of his wonderful stories.
Many people had come to listen.

When evening came, Jesus said to his friends,
"Let's go across to the other side of the lake."

So Jesus and his disciples said goodbye to the people
who'd been listening, and got into their boat.

Then they set sail across the lake.

Jesus felt very tired. He laid his head on a pillow
and fell asleep.

Suddenly, a strong wind blew from the hills.
The little boat was caught in a fierce storm.

*Did the boat
capsize in the
rough weather?*

Stopping a storm

Hard rain fell. Waves tossed the boat backward and forward. The disciples felt *really* scared.

But Jesus was still sleeping peacefully.

The disciples woke him.

"Master!" they shouted. "Please do something to save us – we're all going to drown!"

Jesus stood up.

"Be still!" he said sternly to the wind and the waves.

At that moment, the wind dropped. The waves calmed. Everything was still again.

"Why were you so frightened?" asked Jesus. "I am with you. You can always trust me."

"Who is this? Even the wind and the waves obey him!"

Mark 4:41 CEV

Jesus showed that he could control even the weather.

25

A girl falls ill

*Jairus fell at
Jesus' feet and
begged him
to come to his
house.*

Luke 8:41 NRSV

A man named Jairus lived beside the Lake of Galilee.
One day his little girl fell ill. Jairus knew Jesus healed
people, so he went to find him.

"Please come to see my little girl," Jairus asked.

"I'll come at once," said Jesus.

Then Jairus saw a man pushing through the crowd.

"Don't bother Jesus now," said the messenger.
"Your little girl has died."

Jairus was in
charge of the
synagogue in
Capernaum.

"Don't be scared!" Jesus said
gently to Jairus.
"Just believe in me."
Jesus walked on
with Jairus.

Wake up!

Jesus entered into Jairus's house. He could hear lots of weeping and wailing.

"Please go away!" said Jesus to the people making all the noise. "The little girl isn't dead – she's asleep."

They laughed at him.

Jesus sent them off and then followed Jairus into the room where the girl lay.

Jesus took her hand gently in his warm hands.

"My dear, wake up!" he said.

The girl opened her eyes.

She sat up and looked around. "Find your daughter some food," said Jesus.

Very soon she was feeling much better.

Her parents were astounded.

Luke 8:56 REB

Jesus told Jairus and his wife to have faith that their little girl would get well.

27

A boy's lunch

"We have only five loaves of bread and two fish!"

Matthew 14:17
NLT

Jesus went to the hills for a rest, but a crowd soon gathered. Jesus placed his hands on everyone who was ill. Suddenly, they were well.

After this, Jesus started to tell the crowd some of his wonderful stories. The day went on, and people began to feel tired and hungry.

Jesus' friends asked, "Has anyone brought food?"

"I have five small loaves," said one young boy. "And two little fish. Jesus can have them all!"

Jesus smiled at the boy and took his basket. He blessed the bread and gave it to his friends. Next Jesus divided up the little fish and gave pieces to his friends. The disciples gave out the food to the crowd. More than 5,000 people were there – and everyone had plenty to eat. It was a wonderful miracle!

How could that be enough for everyone?

Dangerous journey

Jesus told many great stories.
This is one of the best loved.

Once a man had to travel from Jerusalem to Jericho
along a lonely road through the mountains.
   Robbers stole everything he had and beat him up.
Then they ran off, leaving him lying injured.
   A priest was walking to Jerusalem. When he noticed
the man on the ground, he crossed to the other side
of the road and walked on.
   Along came a man who helped in the Temple.
As soon as he saw the injured man,
he crossed over too and walked past.

A stranger helps

A third man came along the road.

He was a foreigner, from the land of Samaria.
But he stopped and bandaged the man's wounds.

Then he helped the man onto his donkey,
and took him to an inn.

"Look after my friend!" he told the innkeeper.
"Make sure he has everything he needs."

*Jesus said, "Go
and do the
same!"*

Luke 10:37 CEV

***Does Jesus
want us to help
only people we
know?***

"Which of the three men
acted like a true friend
to the man who was
robbed?" asked Jesus.

"The stranger," came
the answer.

"Yes: the stranger did
exactly what God wants."

One lost sheep

Here is another of the much-loved stories Jesus told.

There was once a good shepherd, who had exactly one hundred sheep. He knew them all by name and loved every one of them.

One night a sheep went missing. The shepherd immediately set out in search of his lost sheep.

At last he found it. He carried the lost sheep home on his strong shoulders.

The shepherd called to his friends.

"Be happy!" he said. "I have found my lost sheep."

Jesus said, "I am like a good shepherd. I care for people who are lost."

"Your Father in heaven doesn't want any of these little ones to be lost."

Matthew 18:14
CEV

Jesus said he came to seek out people who are lost.

A boy leaves home

Jesus told this great story too.

There was once a rich farmer who had two sons.

One day the younger son went to his father.

"Give me my share of your money," said the boy.
"Then I can go off and enjoy myself."

The father gave the younger son his share of his
money. The boy left home and went away to a far
country. He had a great time! But one day the boy's
money ran out.

"You can look after my pigs,"
said a farmer.

So the boy sat with the
grunting, greedy pigs.

After a bit, he began
thinking of his family
back home.

The teachers
of the Law of
Moses started
grumbling,
"This man
Jesus is friendly
with sinners.
He even eats
with them."

Luke 15:2 CEV

This is
often called
"The Parable
of the Prodigal
Son".

33

Jesus said,
"In the same
way, there is
more happiness
in heaven
because of
one sinner
who turns to
God than over
ninety-nine
good people
who don't
need to."

Luke 15:7 CEV

God is always
ready to
forgive us.

The welcoming father

"How stupid I've been!" the boy said to himself.
"There are lots of men working for my father. They
have all the food they need. I'll go home and say,
'Father, I don't deserve to be called your son any more.
Can I work for you instead?'"

So the boy set out on the long walk home.

While he was still a good way off, his father
ran to meet him. He hugged his son.

The boy said, "Dad, I'm so sorry…"

But his father cried, "Cook a feast!
I thought my son was dead – but
he's home again. He was lost
– now he's found. We'll
have such a party!"

Man up a tree

In Jericho, there lived a tax collector named Zacchaeus. He was very rich, because he took more money than he was supposed to. No one liked him.

Jesus was visiting Jericho. Everyone crowded the streets to see him. Zacchaeus wanted to see Jesus too, but he was very short.

He clambered up a sycamore tree and sat on a high branch. Now he would see Jesus too!

Zacchaeus had a big shock. When Jesus reached his tree, he stopped.

"Zacchaeus," Jesus called, "come down! I want to have dinner with you today!"

After Zacchaeus met Jesus, he changed. He became much kinder. "I'll give half my money to poor people," Zacchaeus said.

Zacchaeus was a chief tax collector and was very wealthy.

Luke 19:2 NIV

Zacchaeus probably thought he wouldn't be noticed if he sat in the tree.

*"Bless the king
who comes in
the name of the
Lord!"*

Luke 19:38 NLT

Years before,
the wise men
had realized
that a new
king had been
born. Now the
people saw that
Jesus was king.

Jesus the king

Jesus made a final journey to Jerusalem.

He sat on a young donkey and rode into the city.

The road was filled with people coming to the great festival.

When the crowds saw Jesus, they grew very excited. Some welcomed Jesus as king, spreading out their cloaks on the road before him.

Others cut down branches from palm trees and laid them on the road.

People started shouting with joy.

Soon everyone joined in, chanting: "Hosanna! Hooray for God!" and "Praise God in heaven!"

Love one another

*Jesus said,
"As I have loved
you, so you
must love one
another."*

John 13:34 NIV

In Jerusalem Jesus had a special supper with his disciples. At the meal he said, "One of you eating with me is going to hand me over to my enemies."

Just then Judas crept out. He was plotting against Jesus.

"Love one another, as I have loved you," Jesus told his disciples.

He took some bread, thanked God for it, and broke it. He gave a piece to each of his friends.

Then Jesus took a cup of wine. "Drink this wine!" he said. "The wine is my life. I offer my life for all."

*Who do you
think Judas
was meeting?*

In the garden

Jesus said to them, "I am so sad that I feel as if I am dying. Stay here and keep awake with me."

Matthew 26:38 CEV

After supper, Jesus took his disciples out of the city.
He led them to a garden called Gethsemane,
on the Mount of Olives.

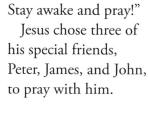

"Wait here," said Jesus.
"I want to pray alone.
Stay awake and pray!"
Jesus chose three of
his special friends,
Peter, James, and John,
to pray with him.

Jesus knew
that Judas was
going to betray
him. He felt
very, very sad.

Asleep!

Jesus went a little further into the garden.
He knelt to pray. He was frightened about
what was going to happen.

"Father, don't let me have to do this!" he prayed.
"But it's not what I want that matters
– it's what *you* want."

Jesus walked back to the three disciples.
They were all asleep. "Peter!" Jesus said, waking him.
"Why are you sleeping? Please watch and pray!"

Jesus went alone into the garden again to pray.
But the disciples went back to sleep.

*Jesus said,
"The time has
come for the
Son of Man to
be handed over
to sinners."*

Matthew 26:45
CEV

*How did Jesus
feel, when
he found
his disciples
sleeping?*

Jesus said to the
chief priests,
"This is your
hour – when
darkness
reigns."

Luke 22:52–53
REB

Judas kisses

"Wake up!" Jesus shouted to his friends. "Here comes
the man who's going to hand me over to my enemies!"

Judas was leading some men carrying swords and
sticks. He had told some priests, "The man I kiss is the
one you must arrest."

Judas walked right up to Jesus and kissed him.

"*Teacher!*" he said.

So the men with Judas knew it was Jesus.

The guards seized Jesus and took him prisoner.

The disciples all ran off. They were very frightened.

Now Jesus was
alone with his
enemies.

Pilate's question

The soldiers took Jesus to the Roman ruler, who was called Pilate.

"Jesus is causing a lot of trouble," priests told Pilate. "You should have him put to death!"

Pilate questioned Jesus carefully.

"I can find nothing wrong with him," he said.

Each year, at this time, he set one prisoner free.

"What shall I do with Jesus?" asked Pilate.

"Put him on the cross!" screamed the watching crowd.

"Have it your way! Take him and crucify him. But don't blame me for Jesus' death."

Jesus told Pilate, "I was born into this world to tell about the truth."

John 18:37 CEV

The priests could not have Jesus put to death: only Pilate could do that.

43

Even as he
was dying,
Jesus asked his
friend John
to care for his
mother Mary.

Three crosses

Roman soldiers marched Jesus away. They took him
outside the city. The guards made him carry a heavy,
wooden cross up a hill.

On the hill they fixed Jesus on the cross.

They also put two robbers on crosses,
one each side of Jesus.

Pilate told the soldiers to nail a sign over Jesus' head.
It said: "Jesus of Nazareth, the king of the Jews."

Jesus' family and his friends
stood sadly nearby.

The sky went dark.

Jesus dies

Jesus cried out, "It is finished!" Then he died.

A Roman captain said, "This really was God's Son!"

Afterwards a good man named Joseph took Jesus' body and wrapped it in a cloth. Then he laid it in a grave carved from rock.

Finally Joseph rolled a huge stone across the doorway of the grave, so Jesus' body would not be disturbed.

Two Roman soldiers stood guard at the door.

Mary Magdalene and Mary, the mother of Jesus, were watching and saw where the body was placed.

Mark 15:47 CEV

Now no one could enter the tomb!

Till this moment they had still not understood the Scripture, that he must rise from the dead.

John 20:9 NJB

Why did Peter and John now believe Jesus had risen from the dead?

Mary's discovery

Early Sunday morning, Jesus' friend Mary went to Jesus' tomb. She was astonished to see the great stone had been rolled back. But she couldn't see Jesus' body!

Mary rushed back into Jerusalem.

"They've taken Jesus' body," she told Peter and John. "I can't find it!"

Peter and John rushed to the tomb.

Peter went straight into the tomb. There was no body! The sheets Jesus' body had been wrapped in were neatly folded.

Immediately Peter and John believed Jesus had risen from the dead.

The gardener?

Peter and John went back into Jerusalem.

But Mary stayed outside the tomb, crying. She peered into the tomb again. Through her tears, she saw two angels.

"Why are you crying?" they asked.

"They've taken away Jesus' body," she answered. "I don't know where it is."

Mary turned around and saw Jesus standing there – but she didn't recognize him.

"Why are you crying?" Jesus asked Mary. "Who are you looking for?"

Mary thought it was the gardener. "If you've taken Jesus' body," she said, "Please tell me where you've put it."

Jesus said, "Mary!"

Immediately Mary knew he was Jesus.

"Teacher!" she said.

Mary Magdalene went to the disciples with the news: "I have seen the Lord!"

John 20:18 NIV

How did Mary Magdalene recognize Jesus?

Day
40

Jesus said, "Go to the people of all nations and make them my disciples."

Matthew 28:19
CEV

After Jesus disappeared, his disciples returned to Jerusalem very happy.

Always!

Forty days later, Jesus' disciples were in a house in Jerusalem. Suddenly, Jesus appeared in the room.

"Don't be afraid!" said Jesus. "Men killed me – but God has brought me back to life."

After this, Jesus walked with them to the Mount of Olives, just outside Jerusalem. As they were standing on the hill, Jesus said, "Now I'm going to be with God. But I am still with you. I always will be."

Then a cloud took Jesus away.

Suddenly, two angels appeared.

"Why are you staring at the sky?" asked the angels.

"Jesus is with God in heaven. One day he will return. Now do as Jesus told you."

48